STAR WARS™

Quotes To Live Your Life By

First published in the UK in 2023 by Studio Press,
an imprint of Bonnier Books UK,
4th Floor, Victoria House, Bloomsbury Square, London WC1B 4DA
Owned by Bonnier Books,
Sveavägen 56, Stockholm, Sweden

www.bonnierbooks.co.uk

Printed in Lithuania
2 4 6 8 10 9 7 5 3 1

Written by Roland Hall
Edited by Emil Fortune
Designed by Maddox Philpot

STAR WARS™

Quotes To Live
Your Life By

STUDIO
PRESS

A long time ago,

in a galaxy far,

far away ....

Try not.

Do. Or do not.

There is no try

YODA

Episode V: The Empire Strikes Back

The object isn't to win. It's just to stay in it as long as you can.

QI'RA

Solo: A Star Wars Story

Get back up.
Always get
back up.

LUKE SKYWALKER

The Book of Boba Fett
Chapter 6: "From the Desert
Comes a Stranger"

You're going to find that many of the truths we cling to depend greatly on our own point of view.

●

OBI-WAN KENOBI

Episode VI: Return of the Jedi

You can't stop the change any more than you can stop the suns from setting.

•

SHMI SKYWALKER

Episode I: The Phantom Menace

Luminous beings are we, not this crude matter.

.

YODA

Episode V: The Empire Strikes Back

Let the

Wookiee

win.

•

C-3PO

Episode IV: A New Hope

Be careful not to choke on your aspirations.

●

DARTH VADER

Rogue One: A Star Wars Story

Always remember: your focus determines your reality.

·

QUI-GON JINN

Episode I: *The Phantom Menace*

I have spoken.

•

KUIIL

The Mandalorian
Season 1, Chapter 1:
"The Mandalorian"

Your eyes can deceive you. Don't trust them.

●

OBI-WAN KENOBI

Episode IV: A New Hope

Nothing's impossible.

•

LEIA ORGANA

Episode IX: *The Rise of Skywalker*

I like firsts. Good or bad, they are always memorable.

•

AHSOKA TANO

The Mandalorian
Season 2, Chapter 13:
"The Jedi"

We don't all have the luxury of deciding when and where we want to care about something.

●

CASSIAN ANDOR

Rogue One: A Star Wars Story

When you ask for trouble, you should not be surprised when it finds you.

●

PLO KOON

The Clone Wars
Season 1, Episode 2
"Rising Malevolence"

The fear of loss is a path to the dark side.

YODA

Episode III: *Revenge of the Sith*

Sometimes there are things no one can fix.

●

PADMÉ AMIDALA

Episode II: *Attack of the Clones*

The ability to speak does not make you intelligent.

QUI-GON JINN

Episode I: *The Phantom Menace*

Hope is like the sun. If you only believe it when you see it, you'll never make it through the night.

•

VICE ADMIRAL HOLDO

Episode VIII: *The Last Jedi*

That's how we're gonna win. Not fighting what we hate... Saving what we love.

ROSE TICO

Episode VIII: *The Last Jedi*

The light will fade, but it is never forgotten.

OBI-WAN KENOBI

Obi-Wan Kenobi
"Part V"

Fear leads to anger, anger leads to hate, hate leads to suffering.

•

YODA

Episode I: *The Phantom Menace*

Of course I'm afraid. But there's a difference between fear and losing your nerve.

CASSIAN ANDOR

Andor
Season 1, Episode 6, "The Axe Forgets"

Some things are stronger than blood.

●

LUKE SKYWALKER

Episode IX: The Rise of Skywalker

Let's keep a little optimism here.

HAN SOLO

Episode VI: *Return of the Jedi*

There are many ways to lead. You just have to find yours.

●

BAIL ORGANA

Obi-Wan Kenobi
"Part I"

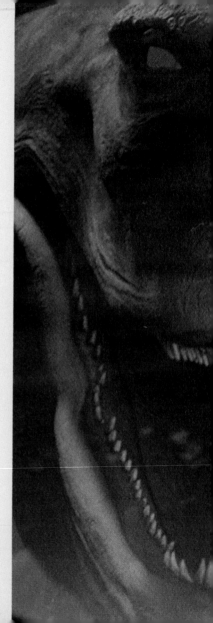

There's always a bigger fish.

QUI-GON JINN

Episode I: *The Phantom Menace*

Yeah, I'm responsible these days, it's the price you pay for being successful.

•

LANDO CALRISSIAN

Episode V: The Empire Strikes Back

Size

matters not.

•

YODA

Episode V: *The Empire Strikes Back*

I'm not leaving my fate up to chance.

DIN DJARIN

The Mandalorian
Season 2, Chapter 9: "The Marshal"

Never

tell me

the odds!

•

HAN SOLO

Episode V: *The Empire Strikes Back*

Let go of
your hate.

•

LUKE SKYWALKER

Episode VI: Return of the Jedi

Don't believe everything you hear.

●

BO-KATAN KRYZE

The Mandalorian
Season 2, Chapter 11: "The Heiress"

A little more knowledge might light our way.

•

YODA

Episode III: Revenge of the Sith

Don't just

blindly follow

the program,

exercise some

free will!

•

L3-37

Solo: A Star Wars Story

Talent without training is nothing.

•

LUKE SKYWALKER

The Mandalorian
Season 2, Chapter 16: "The Rescue"

Some things you can't forget. But you can fight to make them better.

•

TALA DURITH

Obi-Wan Kenobi
"Part V"

Whenever you gamble, my friend, eventually you lose.

•

QUI-GON JINN

Episode I: The Phantom Menace

Pass on what you have learned.

YODA

Episode V: The Empire Strikes Back

All mentors have a way of seeing more of our faults than we would like.

•

PADMÉ AMIDALA

Episode II: *Attack of the Clones*

In my experience, there's no such thing as luck.

OBI-WAN KENOBI

Episode IV: A New Hope

Trust goes both ways.

JYN ERSO

Rogue One: A Star Wars Story

Concentrate on the moment. Feel, don't think, use your instincts.

●

QUI-GON JINN

Episode I: *The Phantom Menace*

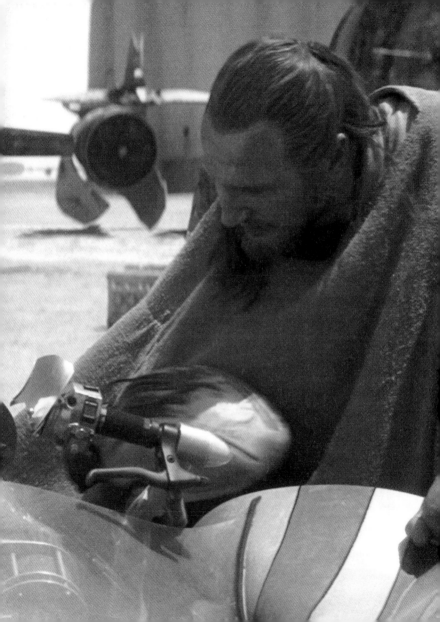

Loyalty and solidarity are the Way.

•

DIN DJARIN

The Book of Boba Fett
Chapter 5: "Return of
the Mandalorian"

Wars not make one great.

·

YODA

Episode V: *The Empire Strikes Back*

Persistence without insight will lead to the same outcome.

•

THE ARMORER

The Book of Boba Fett
Chapter 5, "Return of the Mandalorian"

Be mindful
of your
feelings.

·

MACE WINDU

Episode I: *The Phantom Menace*

Sometimes we must let go of our pride and do what is requested of us.

•

ANAKIN SKYWALKER

Episode II: *Attack of the Clones*

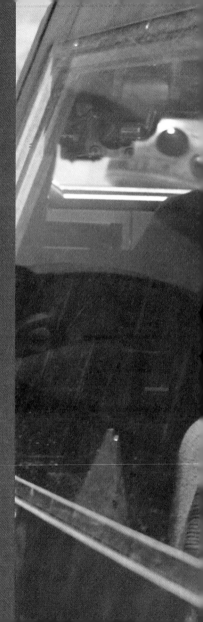

As long as there's light, we've got a chance.

•

POE DAMERON

Episode VII: The Force Awakens

No one's ever really gone.

•

LUKE SKYWALKER

Episode VIII: *The Last Jedi*

The greatest teacher, failure is.

•

YODA

Episode VIII: *The Last Jedi*

Don't get cocky.

•

HAN SOLO

Episode IV: A New Hope

May the Force be with you.

•

LEIA ORGANA

Episode VII: *The Force Awakens*